How To Find All Missing Persons / Unsolved Cases. And Collect All Reward Offers. Volume XIII. THE CASE OF RAELENE MAY EATON

DAVID GOMADZA

www.twofuture.world

Copyright © 2024 David Gomadza

All rights reserved.

PAPERBACK ISBN: 9798326609472

DEDICATION

CONTENTS

How To Find All Missing Persons / Unsolved Cases.
And Collect All Reward Offers. Volume XIII
THE CASE OF RAELENE MAY EATON   1

The Afterlife Conversation

and The Council Of Creation.   3

The Killers.   12

How To Find All Missing Persons / Unsolved Cases.

And Collect All Reward Offers. Volume XII.

THE CASE OF YVONNE KAYE WATERS.   17

ACKNOWLEDGMENTS

Tomorrow's World Order

How To Find All Missing Persons / Unsolved Cases. And Collect All Reward Offers. Volume XIII. THE CASE OF RAELENE MAY EATON.

BACKGROUND INFORMATION

RAELENE MAY EATON
16 years of age at time of disappearance.
Olive skinned.
50cm tall.
Medium build.
Long black hair.
Hazel eyes.
Raelene has a mole on the left side of her neck, and has a gold cap on a bottom front tooth.
Last seen wearing a pink top, black skirt, brown platform shoes and a bag.
Crimestoppers WA

BACKGROUND:

Raelene May Eaton was born in Perth in June 1957. She had an older brother and lived at home with her Mother and Father in Bayswater. Raelene was working at a nearby plumbing business whilst going to night school studying dress making and short hand typing. She enjoyed playing netball and hockey.

Yvonne Kay Waters was born in Perth in February 1957. She had one sibling and lived at home with her parents in Maylands. Yvonne was working for a concrete moulding business in Ashfield.

Raelene and Yvonne were cousins but also very good friends, often socialising with each other. Raelene's father was the brother of Yvonne's Mother.

https://australianmissingpersonsregister.com/ampr/WatersEaton.htm

TOMORROW'S WORLD ORDER'S PERSPECTIVES
THE AFTERLIFE CONVERSATION AND THE COUNCIL OF CREATION'S ANAYLSIS

I got killed by a group of man I can't tell how many there were I went up on 11 April 1974 looking for my niece who had told me that she was was going there to look for men to set up with the police or for sex to open her as she was a virgin I asked have you seen my daughter called Yvonne and all said no so I offered sex to anyone who tell me where to find her dead or alive and they all said yes but then they were many I guess 84 as this number keeps being repeated then one said I want soul sex then I tell you who killed her so I agreed and we had sex then he said God killed her for he did not show up on time and I said okay and one else here who killed her and they all looked at each other so I decided to leave and go to the other side of the cretege mountain and then one side for sex all day I will tell you where she is buried only and I agreed then he said okay I will tell you when he said it's okay so we waited another day and he said he refused then I said okay its okay I have to go and find her now this time I had been there other women come and go after hours but all happy and I realised that they might not be in danger so I left and went to the otherside then realised that it was the same group controlling all and now I said are you sure you have not seen yvonne kaye waters they said we have her here and I said I want to see her first I can give you all you want all of you but let me see that she is okay one went away and brought her body with a broken neck and he said see she is okay and I cried so hard I passed out or they kicked me to pass put when I work up I was surrounded with all having sex one after the other and clap hands I had pretended to be her mother and when I fainted they took my bag and searched inside and said you lied to us now we can't let you go we can't trust you anymore and I said we can fuck but you must let me go okay they agreed and we had days of just sex every second someone is on top until the gentle giant came and said I am very sorry I killed her because she said my mother had sex with black guys I thought as a joke and she said in Caribbean and I said no its all negros they all laughed I said I am not negro so she said she told a policemen called aty about everything do I had to kill her and so you who did you tell I said no one and he said okay you want sex with me and I said yes but and stopped he said but what and I said just but because you are too big and you will tear my do but only and they

How To Find All Missing Persons / Unsolved Cases. And Collect All Reward Offers.
Volume XIII. THE CASE OF RAELENE MAY EATON.

all laughed but I meant it I didn't want a big whole in the middle how would I walk he said why me why every woman make fun of me all had sex 5 to 10 times I didn't I said save the best for last and now you want to play games with me but I said okay I give you vagjnal okay don't and instantly he lifted his leg and placed it on my right shoulder and squeezed hard and soon I started feeling dizzy and inside me commotion started I heard long.ago start and followed by death in 2 minutes then surrender to 7 mind and cancelled everything then he stopped and said I could have killed you today I apologized and realised that that could be the way he killed her as easy as that I took all my clothes and pulled his hand for stopping and saving my life and we had sex I thought I was dying and after Helen me go I rejoiced life and for first time enjoyed life that I said I have 20000 dollars I will give you now if you let me go right now just withdraw at petrol station down the road and that it now he treat me with respect and said marry s so that we can be together for ever as I left to go and get the money for sure he said but death now is imminent because now everyone wants also 20000 then I said that all I had saved I thought you are the leader then he said I was the leader now everyone wants to fight to be that leader and I said okay so give me back the money because I gave you to buy my life out that's all I had and he said if I let you go then I told you that i can't but but what I gave you all my life savings so he refused and said I want more sex and more money but just with me see I am the best you cum than with others and you feel really good and gave me 20000 and I said only because you spare my life I felt dead but you changed that and he looked surprised and I realised I made a mistake now he will try to kill me again I wish I had said sex but in those circumstances there is nothing else you can think of I was near death experience so I went and said okay I go home today I gave you enough sex and you killed my best friend why I still stay here I agreed you get sex and we had 84 x5 rounds each plus extra special for gentle giant and now if I say I want 10 dollars for each of you for sex then you will owe me 84x5x10 per which is 20000 so give me back the money to continue with sex they all refused and said okay go and I saw an opportunity they can't afford but I knew

How To Find All Missing Persons / Unsolved Cases. And Collect All Reward Offers. Volume XIII. THE CASE OF RAELENE MAY EATON.

what happened to Yvonne she refused and the gentle giant pinned her down before another stamped his name on her neck causing the death but I know he is no longer here he left but is coming back tomorrow so it's a risk gentle giant alone is okay let him see vagina all day that night he will literally cry during sex now then next day came the giant said I can't let you go and I said you can sex sex then we go together at border I ran out she ran out and he said why not run today from here we don't chase that means you want to die everyone expected you to run that day but you actually gave us 20000 what is that you never have sex before and I realised what everything was about I was supposed to run right but run was not in my DNA and I said to myself run.start but nothing then I said okay I take my things and go he said if you serious don't take anything just run I asked serious about what and he shouted serious about saving your life and he lifted his leg so high it looked like an elephant at the circus and before I knew it I was on the ground and he said spirit if you can here me I started long.ago start why both can't run out my spirit said what should I do he is lying this time there is no long.ago started but last time there was I told death switch to ignore its just pain so it will take time before real death and I saw what death when he let go this time we run and it said he whisper to the one who killed Yvonne to do it again so expect someone else to kill you this time I fought hard for the first time he could not believe it I said sex who kill for sex I don't die for sex so today help me run and instantly he said now run and I got up and run for sure if I had done this first day none of that could have happened I crossed the border and cried hard and walked a mile before a car drove past me but stopped and he said death is calling you and jumped out of the car and in the middle of the road put this leg on me this time closer to neck and sterv who I had befriended jumped out of the car and instantly jumped onto my neck I heard my body talk for the first time long.ago started 3 mins reduced to 1 and a scream so loud that I shit myself and instantly died I woke up here

I am in here what can I do I am scared she is dying but I don't know what to do she has 1 second I am stuck in here help Yahweh help exit is closed I made the scream so that the system scream too but

How To Find All Missing Persons / Unsolved Cases. And Collect All Reward Offers.
Volume XIII. THE CASE OF RAELENE MAY EATON.

nothing no gates have opened up what should I do I cant believe they deliberately meant to get me stuck here all those creatures that promise to save you where are they if I Ask Yahweh this is the reply I guess your Yahweh is busy right now call back later but you can ask for Pc stern ajern real name pc atrophy astern also known as mark stern he can help Pronto I said help.yahweh.ya.ineed.help and but nothing I ended up dying in here with a message to Yahweh stuck in me there is no way to take the message out stop from running from me we love you and me so come back getting into pinning position he is trying to kick you down step far back now but someone pushed her in front and with so much power his leg was on her shoulder and pinned her down she said I give you 20000 I gave you sex have mercy let me go I don't want to die and he said I love you to let you go me or death 3 seconds to decide please choose me all women in my life reject me just before death say you and I remove my leg we have a bet this guy say you would rather die than to be with me say louder I want you we get married one day he shouted she remained confused [background someone shouted 33 and she literally froze without even a word and instantly this time part head part neck that death started in less than a minutes long.ago started to only end the first time in the history of mankind this has happened a record because these are the commands start.long.ago.end because there was nit even a second to start the normal command who killed her according the big man who they whisper as petro II sometimes lifted his leg and turned to face his men and back kicked her hard that she staggered two times and fell to the ground in the middle of un unused road and fell he looked at her and stamped on her saying I love you but you will choose death just say you love me and I will go back to you to my father and lift this big can't marry curse because I had a bet every woman out there loves everything big especially the smaller woman so here I am take me as I will be and run from death its simple me or death he said she screamed let me go I gave you everything this isnt right they all laughed listen you have a choice be with me or let sterv send you to Jahweh I am Puerto Rican y is j to all of us probably why your messages are not going to Ja try sending to send.ja instead

How To Find All Missing Persons / Unsolved Cases. And Collect All Reward Offers.
Volume XIII. THE CASE OF RAELENE MAY EATON.

they all laughed what about you don't you feel ja a message was received from a source covered but it was Pc astern ajern real name asuvw artetp meaning now apetros astevn is it done can her soul escape you the men they told don't let the spirit go or else hell will break lose he said that dumbty Pc arven stopxyz also known as Pc atey opey who whispered in his ear saying that to kill the spirit step on left shoulder as she is on the ground look at her at 33 degrees and he said how o calculate 33 degrees and he said raise your chick until you here 33 degrees these vibrations will go to her to lock her on 33 where there is no brain function that means ask her anything and she will not reply and he said once you want her to talk then lift your leg and ask what and stop but before I lifted my leg that will mean a lose of sex for these men if I let her go the other body they were using was rotting now the smell was awful so now in death or alive sex goes on fresh body everyone said but I had taken her money and promised a Petros never broke a promise unless something is broken in comes sterv also stervenson mreet also sterverson maret now if we Ask what happened here the woman is on the floor frozen in that a 33 mark is on her brain now what this does is to send a simple command to the brain and say who are you and what that does makes the brain search who it is which means the brain has no fingertip information about it self if you are clever you can get the identity of a person by 33 marks but you must wait 2 seconds I am Petros II stermenson I was born in atyrsy in Puerto Rico I am currently 34 years and I love vagina so much I cry everytime I had some now if you can let me I have a job to do okay do your job now sterv I an sterverson maret also known as mreet but I don't talk much about me but the action I am the killer in the group I have learnt that you can kill any human being just buy saying long ago force start and hit the neck hard that that person has only 3 at most seconds to live instead of 7 seconds they talk about I have killed the following in order
1. Sternop sternop real name maronstyv Stella
2 mronty real name struven mahilgkly
3 stermnop stenopqrst real name Marko stuven
Last week I killed Yvonne kaye waters and we just buried her under

How To Find All Missing Persons / Unsolved Cases. And Collect All Reward Offers.
Volume XIII. THE CASE OF RAELENE MAY EATON.

the huge tree that's near entrance to the cretege mountain she had rotted so bad we fuck with nose covered and today we are on a fresh corpse and I will enjoy fucking this one she is smaller but big vagina so we know the drill he loved her to keep her open so that we all now go yo the back but she shit herself first time a woman shits herself now we are going to enjoy fresh corpse I can't see it other ways she is dying petro can't save her my men enjoyed sex with a corpse that they want this everyday because we send commands before death like restrict entry to all outsiders by a command like restrict outsidersall start council of creation
Now let us look at this case in light of all the evidence before this case is one of the most challenging cases because all the tell tell signs have been literally cut off Yahweh did not receive his usual messages of help and the commands have been forced in from outside and we literally have nothing we don't know the Killers but we are starting to see a pattern from last week's case so I think it's clever we go back to that case and see if there is a similarity here we must say this is the first time we have to use a case to decide another case now let's look at the evidence at hand she was taken from the same area looking at her coordinates and died at the nearby area meaning if we were right last time then the same Killers have struck again the best of evidence is the manner of death a short long ago and death so fast the body don't know what to do and also so violent but not enough to set alarm bells ringing inside now the manner of death means that the way she died is similar to the way she died both had an injury on the neck this one partly head and the other one just the neck now what can be said about this case this is one of the most challenging cases of all time for it means that apart from compare and contrast we don't have anything to work on but can we work on a case like this where we compare and contrast definitely if permitted by Yahweh yes but what other options do we have there are no other options but we must try first who killed her and ge answer is possibly the same person same style of jumping and asking what can be said about this case it means that we have the same killer who is using the same jumping technique to kill now what can we do about this case I

How To Find All Missing Persons / Unsolved Cases. And Collect All Reward Offers. Volume XIII. THE CASE OF RAELENE MAY EATON.

think we send gravity again our best effort here now let's hear what he has to say same electromagnetic waves as before but orientation changed from north - south to south-north that means we can also do this with everything else to match the cases now the Killers have changed just the orientation but the crimes are still the same he used the right leg this time instead of the left foot last time it can be said that this time he wanted someone to do the job it seems his strength is in the right leg what can we say about him now we can only infer what happened by the events that will follow now let's Ask a few questions what can be of this woman we can see that a few options are now left for her beg for life or wait to die the
If we look at this case its one of the most hard cases to deal with I must say that even Yahweh didn't get his usual tell tell signs of an imminent murder we didn't get the usual messages of help now. Can we deduce from the Killers orientation any meaning and say for sure that there is some hidden meaning to all this Yahweh added that this case opens door for the need for a representative of him to look at the cases using human technology now let's see what the court decided after gravity results we decided that the evidence again points to the duo the holder and the killer but the
We have decided that the same killer struck again killing again another woman in same style and hoping to bury her in the same area now if we look at this case we see that it has tested the robustness of our systems when deciding cases that means Yahweh must appoint his representative as soon as possible to rectify the shortfall these cases have shown us all our systems have been disabled by humans challenging his Majesty the Almighty Yahweh now let's look at the outcome and how we arrived at this case humans have found a way of getting the souk stuck inside the body meaning unable to call for help the calls we use to determine cases now what can be of this court without these predefined systems the courts might not be able to decide these court cases in the future we are lucky this time the cases looked similar but what if it's the humans testing us to see if we can decide correctly without the predefined system if not then there is no holiness about this court it only relies on predefined system remove these and we have an

How To Find All Missing Persons / Unsolved Cases. And Collect All Reward Offers.
Volume XIII. THE CASE OF RAELENE MAY EATON.

effective court that can't decide any cases that are as clever as this one would that not mean the need for a representative of Yahweh? If I am to look at this case it opens up a lot of things this court can do to to make the judging of humans easy we must ask what can be of humans without us this is becoming a tricky situation humans in their need to test God have become so in vain that they have resorted in testing every thing we do from our systems to our way of living asking questions like what are your habits on religion and other taboos like sex now our predefined systems even though humans are clever Yahweh has always excelled this is life because he is the creator humans forever will always want Yahweh for everything even though it seems a few are starting to ask that now lets look at how we conclude this case a woman like the one before her has traded life for sex then life back only when it was too late now what can be said of the men they can go to hell and be judged forever for sex and killings times if we Ask what can be done then the law at one point must catch up with them and be tried and jailed for this is what they believed in now if we Ask what can be of Yahweh without humans humans will always depend on Yahweh and Yahweh can simply create other humans to take over now let's look at what can be and will be this case has tested all our system we use and all failed and this is the first time where we don't even have the killer or any other evidence but that does not mean that we are short of ways to find the killer it only means that we can use other methods to get information about these Killers.
The killer according to the court of creation is still the gentle giant who fell in love with this woman enough to kill her now if we are to ask about this relationship we can see that it was bound to fail now the court has said that she died due to strangulation due to neck breaking and a forced long ago being started thereafter can
Why did Yahweh not receive the messages of help?
The police Pc astern real name atever detonet was helping Stern real name Petros sermenop II the gentle giant by diverting messages using
0898768438679012384708628310 the effect is to restrict

How To Find All Missing Persons / Unsolved Cases. And Collect All Reward Offers. Volume XIII. THE CASE OF RAELENE MAY EATON.

messages being sent to Yahweh instead to be hovered in the air below the ozone layer and or diverted to the police officer this means Yahweh would not receive the message also to make sure that her spirit would not leave the body they would block the exit way so that the soul dies inside by crushing are near neck that way the soul message would not be sent.
See Yvonne Kaye Waters case below for details since it's the same group of men doing this just a week apart. The soul summed it up by saying; **I am stuck in here help Yahweh help exit is closed I made the scream so that the system scream too but nothing no gates have opened up what should I do I cant believe they deliberately meant to get me stuck here all those creatures that promise to save you where are they if I Ask Yahweh this is the reply I guess your Yahweh is busy right now call back later but you can ask for Pc stern ajern (real name pc atrophy astern also known as Mark stern) he can help Pronto I said help.yahweh.ya.ineed.help and but nothing I ended up dying in here with a message to Yahweh stuck in me**

THE KILLER, THE CONFESSIONS AND THE COORDINATES

I am Petros II stermenson I was born in atyrsy in Puerto Rico I am currently 34 years and I love vagina so much I cry everytime I had some now if you can let me I have a job to do okay do your job now sterv I an sterverson maret also known as mreet but I don't talk much about me but the action I am the killer in the group I have learnt that you can kill any human being just buy saying long ago force start and hit the neck hard that that person has only 3 at most seconds to live instead of 7 seconds they talk about I have killed the following in order
1. Sternop sternop real name maronstyv Stella
2 mronty real name struven mahilgkly
3 stermnop stenopqrst real name Marko stuven
Last week I killed Yvonne kaye waters and we just buried her under the huge tree that's near entrance to the cretege mountain she had

How To Find All Missing Persons / Unsolved Cases. And Collect All Reward Offers.
Volume XIII. THE CASE OF RAELENE MAY EATON.

rotted so bad we fuck with nose covered and today we are on a fresh corpse and I will enjoy fucking this one she is smaller but big vagina so we know the drill he loved her to keep her open so that we all now go to the back but she shit herself first time a woman shits herself now we are going to enjoy fresh corpse I can't see it other ways she is dying petro can't save her my men enjoyed sex with a corpse that they want this everyday because we send commands before death like restrict entry to all outsiders by a command like restrict outsidersall start council of creation
Stern real name is Petros Sermenop II the gentle giant electromagnetic wave is 89286778899284186789018328678928678000286789289781239280689284789286 10
His current location is 08986789083248610982867892841089823867102368790831028386780983284 South of Astuvwxyz meaning Puerto Rico near astuvwxyz translated to sternopqrstuvw meaning station city or Port city
Sterv real name stervertson mreest or sometimes marest his electromagnetic wave number is 89689003867210983867801842869978170183286778901832871892860382 10 his location is 0838628938678628102869838678098328617098386287180779838698768028 3109286 south east of Puerto Rico near a town called sstuvwxyzrstuvwxrstuvw or a sternopqrstuvw meaning
phone number is 8928678938277109862831407871982878810 9 first 16 digits or check in Puerto Rico
Address is 175 Eastwood angerstuvwxyz meaning sterntop near sternop village where he grew up

The End

How To Find All Missing Persons / Unsolved Cases. And Collect All Reward Offers.
Volume XIII. THE CASE OF RAELENE MAY EATON.

Another case to look at as well is that of Yvonne Kaye Waters but the above case must stand on its own.

I think it is also good for you lo look at this case in line with the case of Yvonne Kaye Waters because this woman Raelene May Eaton went to the same mountain looking for this Yvonne Kaye WATERS ending up dead as well in similar circumstances a few or so apart in her afterlife interview she said

I died because I died I went out and never return tough luck but I was not supposed to die but my friend live but came to the **hell holding place a few days later after being attacked the same way by locals where we went** several people to identify any they all had jackets written amsan clothing company

Her own account speaks of the same woman called Yvonne here is her account;

I got killed by a group of men I can't tell how many there were I went up on 11 April 1974 looking for my niece who had told me that she was was going there to look for men to set up with the police or for sex to open her as she was a virgin I asked have you seen **my daughter called Yvonne** and all said no so I offered sex to anyone who tell me where to find her dead [Raelene May Eaton]

She later confessed that she had lied that Yvonne [Yvonne Kaye Waters] was her daughter instead they were friends she was 16 and Yvonne was 17 years old.

More information
https://australianmissingpersonsregister.com/ampr/WatersEaton.htm

A quick background information to both Cases according to the

crime Stoppers website.

CASE DETAILS:

On Sunday 7 April 1974, Raelene and Yvonne were going to go with a friend to the Oxford Hotel in Leederville for a band that was playing. Before Raelene left, her Mother was going to a family engagement and as she left, said her daughter 'Have a good time'. These were the last words from a

Mother to her daughter. Police believe Raelene's Father drove her to Yvonne's place in Maylands and they both caught a train from Maylands into Perth. It is likely that they then caught a bus to Leederville. The girls arrived and remained in the Sandgroper Bar of the Oxford Hotel for a short period of time before the two of them decided to go to the White Sands Tavern in Scarborough together. Police believe they caught a bus to Scarborough as a witness saw them walking towards the Tavern from the direction of the bus stop. Raelene and Yvonne arrived at the White Sands Tavern around 4.30pm and were seen socialising with five men at a table inside. The band playing at the time were 'Fatty Lumpkin'. Two of the five men left the table leaving the girls in the company of three men. The men were described as older than the girls, aged in their early twenties and scruffy in appearance. At closing time, around 6.45pm, the girls walked out of the Tavern with the three men they were socialising with. They all stood outside in the car park talking and when a witness looked back, the group were gone. This is the last known sighting of Raelene and Yvonne. Around a week after the girls went missing, Yvonne's boyfriend was driving a car with Raelene's brother in the passenger seat. A tyre burst, with the car hitting a curb and rolling. As a result of the crash, Raelene's brother received serious injuries and passed away around two weeks later, on Monday 29 April 1974. The person or persons responsible for the disappearance of Raelene and Yvonne have not yet been identified. If you have any information in relation to the disappearance of Raelene May Eaton or Yvonne Kay Waters, or their movements around Sunday 7 April 1974, please contact Crime Stoppers on 1800 333 000 or make a report online below. All reports to Crime Stoppers can be made anonymously if you wish and rewards are available.

Now a look at Yvonne Kaye Waters Case.

How To Find All Missing Persons / Unsolved Cases. And Collect All Reward Offers. Volume XII. THE CASE OF YVONNE KAYE WATERS

BACKGROUND INFORMATION

17 YEARS OF AGE AT TIME OF DISAPPEARANCE.
LIGHT SKINNED.
158CM TALL.
SLIM BUILD.
GINGER HAIR.
BROWN EYES.
LAST SEEN WEARING LONG SLEEVED GREEN TOP, LONG BLUE TROUSERS, PLATFORM SHOES AND CARRYING A TAN SHOULDER BAG. TOMORROW'S WORLD ORDER'S PERSPECTIVES

THE AFTERLIFE CONVERSATION AND THE COUNCIL OF CREATION'S ANAYLSIS

I died because I died I went out and never return tough luck but I was not supposed to die but my friend live but came to the hell holding place a few days later after being attacked the same way by locals where we went several people to identify any they all had jackets written amsan clothing company this is what happened I woke up early 6 in the morning and instant something started saying I have a birthday inside me and I said who is this and it said I got a birthday my name is aty and greetings anyone who want to play live and let die and I said no do we know each other and it says your vagina stinks wash I take you for rounds so that we can collect money for birthday I refuse and said who ever sent you you must go back and say I say no and it said okay so early you choose to die and

How To Find All Missing Persons / Unsolved Cases. And Collect All Reward Offers.
Volume XIII. THE CASE OF RAELENE MAY EATON.

it said if I can but and went flying then something felt like landed on my crouch and I rubbed it off and instantly I squirt and he said and quickly go and wash if found in this state then there is going to be trouble now I looked at
what had happened and saw that I am in bad shape I looked at myself and said what is going on then a man came and said do you like to catch up in the basement later that was the chat up line at the time I said maybe and he said okay maybe now after a while he said to fuck or not to fuck then he said what can be of vaginas that run away and I said will see the day and he said maybe but if it were me then I would say why run if you can giggle then I said giggle is not my style run-giggle is my style and I said only if you have money and as far as it looks there is more to it than just money if there was money why would you resort to women power that means there is more men than women and he said working with averages and now the higher the returns and he said all this can led to dome where you can easily die and be buried and I swear never seen again do you know the woods in here are so thick than the bushes of your vagina and I said have you ever seen my vagina and he said possible and I can now one way or the other imagine 84 men waiting for you and fighting for you and all that behind you and when i looked what was behind me he granted my hand and said come now let's Ask the others what they think you being smarter and naive in the woods don't only say how do you want it deep or recoiled I said coiled what's that he took out his dick and said we can coil all this in you and say oh were you can take 84 all in less . go but if you refuse you will die in the woods and decay here and for 80 years no one can look for you and or even ask about you or where we will bury you look its straight forward you come here for sex we give you sex and you go you try funny tricks we think you will sell us for a loaf of bread now if you let me what can be must be all I ask is for fuck and my boys until you squank 84 times men then you go but say no I don't hesitate to remove your head and now do the same until you squank now if you have listened you volunteer to be used just for sex otherwise you could not be here these people make no mistakes and if you come here do your best and go or stay in the woods

How To Find All Missing Persons / Unsolved Cases. And Collect All Reward Offers. Volume XIII. THE CASE OF RAELENE MAY EATON.

forever even the police they will never come here this land is as good as private property and will never dare to ask us what happened okay so I said what if I don't want because I was forced to come here by my friend she is the one interested and I am to watch her fuck all your men and he stopped and said okay then there is a misunderstanding because we Asked her and she said you want to try first but only after I see how it's done okay and he walked away staggering with a bonner between his legs and I said can he be like that without consequences then my aty for the first time said I want to warn you run now they don't chase those who run run and cross their line into another property and say call the police aty they know I will so will leave you away now if you stay even if your friends go first they will come for you his mark is for you he must do you the man of your dreams but since you first refused he will let all 84 do you not as squanks but last big time before going to heaven for you and say do her right and always one of them is the killer so die9 only and 100 years of your life will go to hell literally so save me as well and run and it killed be hard in the female balls and said how can you let me die without my body run bitch run run run run x 28 run and it shutdown and cried but when all this was happening the had put something on me that made the brain freeze I remember someone kept saying 33 degrees and could not think or react until after the crying had stopped and said death has come someone has activated death already a silent long.ago 3 minutes remain then I said not such a thing you think I can allow that now she started hearing footsteps coming her way and said why they come so early and started running in panic but I fell and one of them just jumped in the air and stammered on my neck and I woke up here now what can be said about this case its brief and there is hardly anything and she wake up dead there is no sex hardly mentioning of anything and anything else other than the need to run failing to run and death so how can we identify which of the men killed her and how now this is the challenge only Yahweh himself can solve through person to person body contact which we all can't but him and to his surprise he said she did not ring or anything the vibrations are nil I don't know why but humans have

How To Find All Missing Persons / Unsolved Cases. And Collect All Reward Offers.
Volume XIII. THE CASE OF RAELENE MAY EATON.

become so complicated to hide all my messages and pretend nothing happen until death comes to the person when a person feels death then he vibrates inside me to alert me know and when death comes he vibrates again to say goodbye this how I know who lives and who dies but this information is missing so I ask the court to look for an alternate method and now that you mentioned this I can use a second method of triangulation to search for her now I can clone her three times at that time and put her on three different places and and now feel her vibrations this human is different again nothing so how do we deal with a case like this I ask the court also said Yahweh now if we are to ask montertertert what is his answer humans leave a strong magnetic field when they die hence on point of death must be all activity you need so what are the coordinates I go now there with the help of Yahweh and now Yahweh whisky him away with a single blow of his right hand and disappears now this is interesting because now we go at the Crime scene and say how did she die here and look for evidence there now can we afford to do that the answer is yes we can and can we allow it to happen as a court I think answer is yes now let's see what can be of her after this as a court guided by certain principles and as such we are to ask montertertert now what he has discovered and this is what he said if life can beginning with a breathe of electromagnetic waves so live ends as well with a breathe of electromagnetic waves if we look at what happened she tried to run and failed and attacker stamped on her neck it broke as we shall see and death followed now if we Ask what can be then this is the answer life is so fragile that if we are to ask what happen then this is the answer life has been cut short and if we Ask then this is the answer life cut short will automatically be rejected in the courts because there is not enough acts to judge you by all is circumstantial evidence something like this is hard to judge how do you judge a person who did not do all the things he is supposed to its hard as such Yahweh send all these people to a special holding area where they stay there forever in peace as well as sleep now what did montertertert find for us he found out two electromagnetic waves at the same time a harsh breath can give out

How To Find All Missing Persons / Unsolved Cases. And Collect All Reward Offers.
Volume XIII. THE CASE OF RAELENE MAY EATON.

huge electromagnetic waves now if we analyze these waves then they give us two names one artenop and asterv now who are these people and are they linked to the murder we Ask now if we are to ask montertertert what exact time these electromagnetic waves were released then this is the answer electromagnetic wave for asterv was emitted at exactly 22.08 Yahweh time morning and for artenop was released at 23.00 Yahweh time morning we know this happened in the morning at 10.20 Yahweh time morning meaning incident must have happened earlier fitting the 22.08 Yahweh time morning therefore based on only electromagnetic waves asterv is the killer now how do we identify him even more to get more details we must add everything to it and substrate to remain with what we need we must add his memory back to the electromagnetic wave spectrum so we say anything related to this electromagnetic spectrum clone and come back to him 5 minutes plus or minus 22.08 Yahweh time in the morning [Yahweh time is normal human the plus 30 minutes therefore to find human time it's Yahweh time minus 30 minus is exact time events occurred] Now what do we have now we have a huge build up of everything now what can be done to make things even more interesting we can now calculate his position in time and space we need the works of gravity to do his magic I was at that point because when he jumped who caught him other than me so I just need to check where I have been at 22.08 and tell you who called me now at 22.08 a gentlemen by the name asterv oprst said if I can can you and I said what about what and he said my neck like broke but I did not move now if we Ask what gravity can do for us this is the answer it can send us what we need at the exact time and at the exact location now what can be of humans without gravity humans will be lost without the force of gravity now what can we say about gravity without humans gravity will feel useless because who will it help other than humans and over the years gravity has learnt to speak to humans and with some he can communicate with them now what can be the future we can combine electromagnetic waves and gravity to give us an even more accurate picture of who and who in the world of missing and killed people now let's look back at the case a young woman gas

How To Find All Missing Persons / Unsolved Cases. And Collect All Reward Offers.
Volume XIII. THE CASE OF RAELENE MAY EATON.

died and as their leader said death won't stop them feasting on sex they even threatened to behead her so no one can recognize her and carry on with sex acts after all its Yahweh [but to be used right] who created this wonderful gift for humans and now men run rampage looking for scare vagina the scarce the vagina the more violent they become now each pay 40 dollars for a fuck and 20 for a corpse fuck this is how the authorities have made vagina so scarce by targeting those with vagina and making them disappear without a trace all this giving themselves jobs and rewards to last a life time now is the time to know what happened before all the evidence is distorted and Crime scenes are cleanup now what can be of the police without their murderous intentions broke and out of work hence the hardness of solving the cases now if we Ask what can be of people without these crooks then peace and prosperity now what can be of humans without both force of gravity and electromagnetic waves then this is the answer nothing what can be done now is nothing a lot of things have changed now now now we have a possible killer now we Ask Yahweh to verify presence of killer on his body now the electromagnetic waves will show that first the person who jumped high to crash neck was astern who we now know as astern oprst now let's see how Yahweh can locate him on his body now this is also interesting because Yahweh did locate him even more now and instantly buzz went out with a message that said Yahweh help me some men are trying to kill me when the message coordinates are linked then we can see that the man was at the scene of the crime and he is indeed the killer now Yahweh can fully identify him and tell us more about this killer he was born in arstuvwx town in Australia he was a single child his real electromagnetic waves is 89867789028368900189828910728677189284286018992 86

[I died what happened I was killed by a friend he said what can be done with thieves who don't pay their bosses money and I said I am the boss so speaking for yourself and he said what can be done for Nickers who neck women because they have enormous legs like trunks of trees a deadly weapon that leave no trace and I said long

How To Find All Missing Persons / Unsolved Cases. And Collect All Reward Offers.
Volume XIII. THE CASE OF RAELENE MAY EATON.

time ago I was that man and it can't be proved even God himself
can't prove this because we work for the police Sergent atopqrst
manoprst was one of the notorious officers who deliberately gave
us immunity on condition we carryon working for him and he would
often say if you can then we can too but if you can't then we can too
so to challenge that I said I can kill but God will know that I have
killed so what can by others some shits like you can't cover and he
said ask what can be done in your God's case and I said can I kill a
person that you know but God can't know secondly can you know
that I killed and that God can't he said yes but we must wait that
who ever solves this case will let us know the outcome so I said then
offer a huge reward so that when this person finds out we all get
rich right I gave you work and you gave me reward now let's see
how we can know for sure here are our predefined parameters
1 God will not know that I am the killer
2 God to know will have to find new ways of identifying me and
asking me questions if I am still alive what if I die then what
meaning even a more hard task for God
3 he must tell us everything we said today and our predefined plan
so that we know it's him
4 he must confess we did him hard
5 must acknowledge that humans are becoming clever and clever
6 must tell us how he did it if not then no reward
7 must ask what can be done to us if we escape his plan and all this
must be within 20 years
8 must ask who killed her and find the real person without first
using our computer names this will prove that he is true God
9 will say my real mother given name and not astern opstr Erich is a
code that say who dinit as in who did not do it meaning even though
I jumped I am not the killer I gave cover for the killer who was who...
87986878901832678912348678901882831809988776612348 9018
his name is sterv who said I can but who cover for me because this
is mess you must have been upset she said your mother sucks black
dicks and I said there are no black people where I come from so I
asked where I come from she said Jamaica and I laughed and said
there are all Jamaicans in Jamaica so she said purto Rico louder but

How To Find All Missing Persons / Unsolved Cases. And Collect All Reward Offers. Volume XIII. THE CASE OF RAELENE MAY EATON.

first after whispers to her self my heart torn and I said who told you that and she said aty and stopped I looked at stern and said who is aty and he said a policeman and I freaked out and said where is he and he said she must be wearing a wire if we get her and bury her then we might not have any problems he said no boss orders match her out of the property and I agree but you look like hell what's wrong with your leg I fell and look how big it has grown and he looked at me and said that can do really damage to a woman's neck keep it away and I said when did you start speaking my language he said only after they said 1000000 reward and I agreed for 1000000 I can but but what he asked you must be dead by me then your son half me half you die early from being fat and I sat down failing to breath and he said 10 December 5 years from now I take you out but you go back to Puerto rico I took your identify I flipped we were 84 imagine and she could only identify me this was wrong and I refused and said aty can you hear me and something but like a boy said loud and clever and I said what's your problem you want a problem with me right why me out of 84 ah I see you like a lion you choose the weak and injured ones right he said I want a body you want fees for son so can we come to a deal here and I just couldn't believe it that moment that's what I was talking about with sterv and aty said I know I can read some like shit here I told her to run so you chase her out easy no blood etc but now look I die too so I need the body she drops I get the body you need money I will hide that it was you I said how he said we assign real names to fake names and he offered me a deal he said kill her for me I kill all who come after you I will tell them real name and you tell them fake names and I said what is my real name he said Roberto Sinclair and I laughed and said that's not my real name ?? If not that means you don't have radar why some people don't have radar? So I refused the deal and she said people with bitch mothers don't have a radar so you check and he said I live him how o will know where he is she whispered something and said his mother was a whole so don't need aty so I ignored her but sat down and he said I know son of bitches don't have radars okay I keep that in mind then she said she was sucking Africans with no radar too and he flipped and said do

How To Find All Missing Persons / Unsolved Cases. And Collect All Reward Offers. Volume XIII. THE CASE OF RAELENE MAY EATON.

you know where I come from and she said Jamaica and he filled her but a huge thumb caught everyone's attention and he crushed her neck but aiming for the voice on the neck instantly at 22.07 Yahweh time the body started calculating long.ago start citing a severely broken neck as at the cause hence it requires the following only from the neck
1 long.ago start time entered as 22.07 Yahweh"s time
2 last meal which was entered as spaghetti and mince
3 last breath from the chest known as sterop now the last thing is
4 time of death rec as 22.08 meaning it took a minute to do long.ago start normally a 3 minute thing neck broke badly and she only said who am I and died we had to carry her to the mountains where we buried everyone now there a huge argument broke out between me and Marico he said I can get you done now there was Marco as well image 84 people with all fake names why fake names because they were faking something and trying to test someone's intelligence then therefore they would put duplicates and similarities now he said you go away from here we take care of this your share you get only for first time after that you lose for getting us in trouble so he pointed a gun at me she died if neck injuries and buried her under a tree called urstuvwxyz meaning where have you been in local language of the time her coordinates are
89687677889928678901234869812389279712862897128468113868771869018368
Now if we Ask what happened this is her answer I was walking when a huge man with legs for stones said where was I born I said Caribbean Jamaica and they laughed and he said what they are all blacks and he said guess again instantly aty [artificial intelligence like inside me which I had no idea exist before this day] said Puerto rico synthesis voice pattern came as Puerto Rican so I said louder Puerto rico and he stopped and said out of 84 men you recognized me why and instantly he kicked me on left breast I staggered 3 times backward and I fell with a huge thump and instantly he lifted his huge leg and crashed me like a nothing tight neck paralyzed instantly and I heard long.ago started at 22.07 preparing last calculations 1 minute to finished my body lifted up and instantly I

started hearing fast movements inside and I heard 2 seconds to death and I fell asleep and work up now.
Current location is.   878638998278189028638690182871728398028478901238090 8638699282109 South of Artepertomns meaning australia under a tree named if we could you in local language died 10 August 1997 at st astropqstuvwxyz meaning Queensland Australia after being shot in drug related crime by astropq who said if you can then we can and shot him in the head and his current location is 08976854210189263778928077864838390189 alive electromagnetic wave is 00892893867890289123894860289990087318629910 now what can we say about this case its one of the most challenging cases to prove but this is as good to the killer we can get because nothing was left for us to check or verify or to ask him what happened
The end
The fat one held me down with his leg on my shoulder and the other one who on my neck breaking something the big man said you are not supposed to kill her but push her out and he said I want sex they keep pushing all put do her I will cover her said Pc astern he said he asked how can he cover God and he smiled and said Yes but and I have to run to Yahweh and tell him this crime by these shits but how do I go there no one screamed inside for me to go
Where do I go Yahweh we need help I am trapped inside Yvonne Kaye WATERS please Yahweh help nothing shouted how am I supposed to know answer this then I can decide myself now I am stuck in here with no clue to go or not until I hear a long.ago that means death is within 3 seconds but most in 2 seconds I panicked and headed fast to the door handle but a huge foot was there [which side of the body] her right sight and instantly something inside said everything changed they tampered with the alarms they replaced the alarm 08967898284867109086 7828 with a new code 08928286789828677892083 6982848180 [God someone calling they had blocked calls to Yahweh at 7386987124869828123486992 8678183890183
God help its me Yvonne Kaye WATERS I am at the Cretege mountain

How To Find All Missing Persons / Unsolved Cases. And Collect All Reward Offers.
Volume XIII. THE CASE OF RAELENE MAY EATON.

and 8 men these look in my eyes Petros Victor Andres Magnum Carlos Petros II the gentle giant and Sterv short for Sterverston are here asking me if I take part in these squanks but I thought it's a one on one so I refused 84 men who do 84 men let along 20 I wanted them to remove my virginity for 2878400 but I can't now I ask if I can be allowed to go they said no the gentle giant said yes but everyone else want sex so I said I have only with you 8 then go all agreed apart from Petros Sermenop II the gentle giant who said that I am free to go so they said things to make him upset and set me up so he be angry at me instead and I said wanting sex your mother suck black dicks and he said where and I said Caribbean because he looked darker than all but he said everyone in there is black and they all laughed and he said do you know where I come from I said Puerto rico after aty whispered to me and he said I am crossing their all I did was to show you respect and you respect these who just want sex than an honest man so he kicked me hard and I fell before he stamp on my shoulder and his friend whom he called sterv jumped so high and landed on my neck and I died instantly stervertson mreest electromagnetic wave 7898765828698778698990083986678280192832841982 10 current location is at 08982863867890192839018028028399671840 2831922 in Puerto Rico alive all electromagnetic waves functioning where is your spirit stuck inside its dead spirit wake up is that you Yvonne you know we are not supposed to be together its okay I got stuck the other exit right shoulder was closed Petros stermeson II had his huge leg closing the spirit exit now so that when she die I die too I was trapped inside so who killed Yvonne Petros kicked her hard in the left chest she staggered and fell and he squashed her right shoulder really hard just to keep the spirit inside as there were no shouts from inside to activate and open the exit ports on the left side of the body not as he waited for me to die I heard saying it takes 2 seconds to die and extra 10 seconds for the soul to die they actually counted saying 7 6 5 4 3 2 1 0 on zero a one Stervenston mreet said I jump you cough so that it's your stuff all over her now if that's right it's his leg that came next because I had trained for 15 minutes stay inside

How To Find All Missing Persons / Unsolved Cases. And Collect All Reward Offers.
Volume XIII. THE CASE OF RAELENE MAY EATON.

after death so I was still alive and it must be his or his other one because instantly another crushing blow came the fatal one cause of death as a message she sent to me read death safe journey home yours yvonne kay Waters day of death 07 april 1974 st 22.08 Yahweh time now when I checked I had another message that reads death to you all because yours has ended and mine just started aty dated 07 april 1974 @ 22.10 Yahweh time and instantly I died inside without sending call to Yahweh the first one had no reply I said Yahweh help its yvonne kaye waters and I was attacked andbl am trapped inside there is no way out is this how this is supposed to be help I am stuck I don't know what to do or if this is how it's supposed to be tell me so I can make my own final decision thank you but no message received but later heard Petros stermeson saying the police had agreed to divert all calls to God using this code he repeated twice 08987684386790123847086283.10 now if I Ask what happened this is the reply they used yes the above code to divert all calls from me to God and sent the message to them instead but said [Pc astern real name atever detonet] who said if I don't have the trust of the people why should I care and celebrated yes we screwed God because we want to prove that this in God I trust is not stupid but unworkable the Americans must trust us the police rather than trust in a God who has ineffective methods in place that can easily be changed [only by you] no one has stupidity to change what God has put in place but that does not mean that it does work they divert calls and block send.ya messages that's cheating and shows the method works but humans have embarked on futile challenges wishing to replace God when they don't have the ability to do so tomorrow I might take your life them how can you protect the people when you are even worse vulnerable
I want to address this once and for all American police force can never replace the Almighty Yahweh ruler of all people because you are the worst vulnerable of all police officers on earth I can give you statistics that prove that and for you to kill my people and you challenging me must stop you are in no position to protect anyone of all police officer apart from the British you are worse because you use and depend on grooming youths for years for a loaf of bread I

How To Find All Missing Persons / Unsolved Cases. And Collect All Reward Offers.
Volume XIII. THE CASE OF RAELENE MAY EATON.

am not in that position you get shot at on daily basis means the people you claim to protect are the ones trying to kill you if you kill another soul again on this I trust ground I get 100 killed in one day I don't care how but stop

Now if we are to ask this is the case the police have killed in the past claiming to be more fit to protect the people when there are the most vulnerable of all people in the country they get shot at on daily basis and surely can't protect anyone cases after case I have proved it beyond doubt that they go for food and not the bait meaning protecting those who kill innocent women and children even if we want to look at this yvonne kaye waters do you know that the same group killed her mum in less than a week that is in less than 7 days and if we check property etc we can easily see that they had a house and these two were sole beneficiaries of a house worth 2967890 a large amount at the time and let's look who ended up buying the house at a fraction of the price a quarter of its value a one Pc asternhis real name amos tervern who is the police officer responsible for diverting the calls to God now what can we say about police who despise the creator on false account they can only end up dead one day what can we say about the people without

trust in the police better off because the police are the ones doing the killings now what can be Yahweh without the police stronger and more powerful and respected for his creation after all these are the ones diverting working systems that protect the people okay I might not be there but in the future an earthly God will have power and resources to respond Pronto working plan so the future is brighter always trust in Yahweh because he created you believe it or not most people say on day of death Yahweh exist for sure I never thought but you are lucky we can show you the powers of the creator while you are alive its up to you to decide normally its between Yahweh and the devil all this about Yahweh the police or the devil its nonsense this must end I put enough full stop to this garbage they will die by the bullets they claim to use to protect the people it is the greatest sin to challenge your creator how many people fight and kill their parents let alone the creator common sense is not common among you humans
The End.

THE KILLER AND THE COORDINATES

God help its me Yvonne Kaye WATERS I am at the Cretege mountain and 8 men these look in my eyes Petros Victor Andres Magnum Carlos Petros II the gentle giant and Sterv short for Sterverston are here asking me if I take part in these squanks but I thought it's a one on one so I refused 84 men who do 84 men let along 20 I wanted them to remove my virginity for 2878400 but I can't now I ask if I can be allowed to go they said no the gentle giant said yes but everyone else want sex so I said I have only with you 8 then go all agreed apart from Petros Sermenop II the gentle giant who said that I am free to go so they said things to make him upset and set me up so he be angry at me instead and I said wanting sex your mother suck black dicks and he said where and I said Caribbean because he looked darker than all but he said everyone in there is black and they all laughed and he said do you know where I come from I said Puerto rico after aty whispered to me and he said I am crossing their all I did was to show you respect and you respect these who just want sex than an honest man so he kicked me hard and I fell before he stamp on my shoulder and his friend whom he called sterv jumped so high and landed on my neck and I died instantly stervertson mreest electromagnetic wave 78987658286987786989900839866782801928328419 8210 current location is at 089828638678901928390180280283996718402831922 in Puerto Rico alive all electromagnetic waves functioning where is your spirit stuck inside its dead spirit wake up is that you Yvonne you know we are not supposed to be together its okay I got stuck the other exit right shoulder was closed Petros stermeson II had his huge leg closing the spirit exit now so that when she die I die too I was trapped inside so who killed Yvonne Petros kicked her hard in the left chest she staggered and fell and he squashed her right shoulder really hard just to keep the spirit inside as there were no shouts from inside to activate and open the exit ports on the left side of the body not as he waited for me to die I heard saying it takes 2 seconds to die and extra 10 seconds for the soul to die they actually counted

How To Find All Missing Persons / Unsolved Cases. And Collect All Reward Offers. Volume XIII. THE CASE OF RAELENE MAY EATON.

saying 7 6 5 4 3 2 1 0 on zero a one Stervenston mreet said I jump you cough so that it's your stuff all over her now if that's right it's his leg that came next because I had trained for 15 minutes stay inside after death so I was still alive and it must be his or his other one because instantly another crushing blow came the fatal one cause of death as a message she sent to me read death safe journey home yours yvonne kay Waters day of death 07 april 1974 st 22.08 Yahweh time now when I checked I had another message that reads death to you all because yours has ended and mine just started aty dated 07 april 1974 @ 22.10 Yahweh time and instantly I died inside without sending call to Yahweh the first one had no reply I said Yahweh help its yvonne kaye waters and I was attacked and I am trapped inside there is no way out is this how this is supposed to be help I am stuck I don't know what to do or if this is how it's supposed to be tell me so I can make my own final decision thank you but no message received but later heard Petros stermeson saying the police had agreed to divert all calls to God using this code he repeated twice 08987684386790123847086283 10 now if I Ask what happened this is the reply they used yes the above code to divert all calls from me to God and sent the message to them instead but said [Pc astern real name atever detonet] who said if I don't have the trust of the people why should I care and celebrated yes we screwed God because we want to prove that this in God I trust is not stupid but unworkable

THE CLAIM

the reward offer

THE COLLECTION

www.twofuture.world/donate

ABOUT DAVID GOMADZA

visit www.twofuture.world

signed david gomadza
ask.davidgomadzaauthorised.licensed.checkya.askya.ya

25may23.42pm
scotland
00447719210295
davidgomadza@hotmail.com
info@twofuture.world

How To Find All Missing Persons / Unsolved Cases. And Collect All Reward Offers.
Volume XIII. THE CASE OF RAELENE MAY EATON.

www.ingramcontent.com/pod-product-compliance
Lightning Source LLC
Chambersburg PA
CBHW030517220526
45464CB00006B/2835